M000086811

God's
Grace
through
Grief

To Sister Hockenhull

Rev. Edward R. Knox, D.Min.

PriorityONE
publications
Detroit, MI USA

God's Grace Through Grief
Copyright © 2012 Edward R. Knox, D.Min.

All rights reserved. No part of this publication may be reproduced, stored in a retrieval system, or transmitted in any form or by any means – electronic, mechanical, photocopy, recording, or any other – except for brief quotations in printed reviews, without the prior permission of the publisher.

All scripture quotations, unless otherwise indicated, are taken from the Holy Bible, New International Version®, NIV®. Copyright ©1973, 1978, 1984, 2011 by Biblica, Inc.™ Used by permission of Zondervan. All rights reserved worldwide. www.zondervan.com

The "NIV" and "New International Version" are trademarks registered in the United States Patent and Trademark Office by Biblica, Inc.™

*Priority*ONE Publications
(800) 596-4490 Nationwide Toll Free
E-mail: info@p1pubs.com
URL: http://www.p1pubs.com

ISBN 10:   1-933972-27-0

ISBN 13: 978-1-933972-27-5

Edited by Patricia A. Hicks

Cover and interior design by Christina Dixon

Printed in the United States of America

Endorsements

Dr. Edward Knox has put his finger on some of the critical issues people face when they have lost their loved one. In this book he points out to his readers that grief is normal and healthy, but it is the way one responses to grief.

Dr. Knox looks at grief and bereavement in the church as well as in the Bible. He also points out to his readers where the image of grief can be found in the Bible. Dr. Knox gives the reader several definitions such as, "Grief is our reaction to loss."

In addressing the problem of grief, Dr. Knox gives readers the correct and the incorrect way to grieve. He reveals to pastors and counselors how they should counsel a grief stricken person or family. In addition, he reveals how grief and bereavement issues should be resolved.

I recommend that all pastors and counselors, as well as church leaders, read *God's Grace through Grief*. It would also benefit funeral home owners and their employees. Dr. Knox directs us to take our grief to the Lord Who is able to see us through our grief experience. It is a book worth buying and reading.

Reverend Dr. Joseph R. Jordan, D. Min

I can't express the elation I feel at this outstanding inspirational book focusing on handling grief. None of us escape the pressures of losing someone; pressures of losing someone precious and meaningful to us and suddenly, without warning we are confronted with grief in its most profound dressing.

We all handle it differently and manifest outwardly various elements of relief. Sometimes we do so and regain our balance in a short period and others take considerably longer. Dr. Knox's direction brings to light all facets of this very complex emotion and enable anyone to grasp something that can help comprehend where you are and how to embrace a solution that places us at peace with the loss.

This is a must read for all of us and I will certainly encourage my friends and relatives to consider what they will do and seek answers in your book. Magnificent literature.

Andre' L. Lee, DPA, FACHE, Hospice President

Move over grief experts! *God's Grace through Grief* is a excellent tool of reference to have in your library. Dr Knox's book is a valuable resource for psychologist, psychiatrist, medical doctors, counselors, clinicians and grievers alike. This book is not only practical but historical, theological as well as, Biblical. With his 5-F theory of the grief process, Dr. Knox gives the readers the 21st century model for recovery much like Kubler-Ross. I contend the griever can recover if they face, feel, fuel, and then ultimately free their grief through faith in God.

Dr. Edward Roberts, MD

Table of Contents

Acknowledgements

I give Honor to God the Creator, praise to Jesus my Savior and glory to the Holy Spirit my Sustainer for protecting, providing, preparing, and anointing me for this ministry. This document is written in loving memory of my son, Marlon DuJuan Holmes, whose spirit lives in all of us who loved him.

And now to my immediate family; words cannot express the emotions I feel as I write for my mother, Mary Knox, who has supported me all of my life, my sisters Fredia, Harriet, Cheryl, and Barbara, and my brother, Fred. To my blessed children, Saran, Rakahn, Siedah and grandchildren, Bria, and Jeremiah, I love you. And finally, to my wife, friend, mother of my children and the anchor that holds the family together, Dranoel, I thank God for your love and support for 39 years. I love all of you, may God bless you all.

⊹⟩━◉⟨━⊹

This book is dedicated to the memory of Maurice, Mark and Marlon.

Introduction

In viewing my life over the last 48 years, I was amazed to see how much grief is a part of everyday living. At the tender age of five the death of my best friend, my puppy (Teddy), presented a feeling that was hard to explain. That feeling was grief. Although I experienced the death of my puppy at an early age, it was years later, after the death of my first son and my father, that I began to experience and understand the reality of a grief experience.

Grief is a normal healthy response to loss. Grief is a person's internal experience. For many, grief is identified with the emotions and feelings related to the experience of a great loss. Bereavement is the external expression of one's grief. Millions of people grieve daily for various reasons and I am one of them.[1]

I was thrust painfully into this arena of grief and bereavement by the death of my first son, Maurice, in 1972, followed by the death of my father in 1973. Subsequently, the pain continued over the years until the death of my second son in 2000. It was in that year I sought assistance for my past and present grief issues.

---

[1] "Grieving: Facing Illness, Death and Other Losses"; available from http://familydoctor.org/ handouts/079.html; Internet; accessed 3/4/2003,11:00 a.m.

I finally realized that I was suffering from unresolved grief for more than 20 years. After the death of my second son I received the effective professional counseling needed to help process and resolve my grief.

Furthermore, after discovering grief can be resolved through a process, I questioned if other grievers understood that process. When death occurs, the question usually asked is "why?" However, after the death of my second son, Marlon, for me the question became "what?" What are you going to do about it, Edward? In fact, what does God want from me? I sought God for an answer. After prayerfully seeking an answer from God, the LORD revealed to me my assignment for the next couple of years. God's will and my purpose for this chapter in my life were being manifested through my grief experiences.

Finally, I took on the awesome task of researching grief and bereavement in various areas such as in the church, in funeral homes and the griever's home. As a direct result, this led to the development of this project, which includes grief workshops and a grief and bereavement guide (brochure) to ensure other grievers would have a guide to assist them through their process of grief.

Thus, it is my goal to address an area of ministry that has been overlooked, neglected, and in many cases underestimated and misunderstood. It is my prayer that the project will assist the griever in their grief process, which will eventually allow the griever to face their grief, feel their grief, fuel their grief, move toward freedom from their grief, as they live out a life of faith after grieving.

Faith dictates the outcome of God's grace. When we exercise our faith God will complete the process. As a result, facing, feeling, fueling and freeing grief is not in our hands. In fact, it is where it has always been – in God's grace.

CHAPTER ONE
The Need

One of society's greatest problems is the drastic need for grief education. It is through education that many of the bereaved are prepared to cope with death. Death is a universal experience shaped by the values and attitudes of the culture, which depends on the particular time and place. More importantly, value structures, religious beliefs, age, ethnicity, and the mode of death impact how a person experiences grief.

In the view of some cultures, grief is expressed in different ways to provide closure. Consider the Asian way of grief. The Japanese ritual of responding to death is usually referred to as "ancestor worship" in English. It is a series of rituals performed by survivors lasting between 33 and 50 years after someone has died. Rituals for the first 49 days accomplish grief work.[2]

The Muslim perspective of grief is different. The Qur'an says "every soul shall have a taste of death: and only on the Day of Judgment shall you be paid your full recompense." In this

---

[2] Dennis Klass and Robert E. Goss, "Asian Ways of Grief," in Hospice Foundation of America, *Living With Grief: Who We Are, How We Grieve* (Washington, DC: HFA Publications, 1998).

culture, parents talk about death, teachers talk about it, and poets write about it. It is part of culture and faith.[3]

In many older European traditions, there has been a custom of having the close relatives each throw a shovel full of earth on the casket at the internment. In South American traditions, they celebrate the dead with a weeklong celebration. In Middle Eastern traditions, grief was often suppressed. In African traditions, the corpse is carried through the community, and the celebration (bereavement) can last from 6 months to a year.

Even in America, the younger generation will pour a libation of an alcoholic beverage on the ground or the grave of the dead as a memorial. Although the traditions are different, for many the results are therapeutic.

Although many ethnic groups grieve out of tradition or their cultural experience, I contend that many do not know how to process grief within their culture simply because grief has been misunderstood. Many traditions may be considered outdated or taboo. In many cultures, people have not been taught, exposed to the methods, or are not familiar with the grief process. What we are taught are usually myths. Therefore, the need for grief education increases.

According to Dr. Diane Hudson, we need to be aware of culture, language and communication modes, physical environment, appearance, worldview, family lifestyles, including social interaction and kinship, religious orientation, educational factors, and food uses.

---

[3] Shukria Alimi Raad, "Grief: A Muslim Perspective," in Hospice Foundation of America, *Living With Grief: Who We Are, How We Grieve* (Washington, DC: HFA Publications, 1998).

As I began researching grief and bereavement, I was reminded of my own culture, language, religion, family lifestyle, education and personal experiences in grief and loss over the years. The major differences are maturity, family lifestyle, religious faith, and education. What I was taught or not taught impacted my perspective on life, death, and grief.

As I reflected upon the death of my six-month-old son during my teen years, I was told, "don't worry, every thing will work out. You can have more children." Clichés and myths do not resolve the pain and suffering. Neither does it help bring resolution or recovery from grief. In fact, I was never exposed to the grieving process or taught how to grieve. Unfortunately, I never had the opportunity to grieve until 30 years later. Furthermore, the loss of my 24-year-old son in my mid-forties provoked me to take a closer look at how to effectively recover from grief. Ultimately, this helped me realize the need for more research and resources available in the area of grief and bereavement. I contend that, as a community, we need to be prepared to assist in this critical area of grief.

Historical

The history of grief can be traced back as far as the beginning of creation. In primitive times, death was viewed as a natural occurrence. It was expected and accepted by many cultures and religions, which made grief and bereavement easier to cope with.[4]

---

[4] Charles Zastrow and Karen K. Ashman, *Understanding Human Behavior and the Social Environment* (Chicago, Illinois: Nelson Hall Publishing, 1995).

In Biblical times, the term often used to represent grief was "mourning," which shared a variety of customs including weeping and screaming in an excessive manner; wearing dark-colored garments; songs and shouts of lamentation; funeral feasts; hired mourners; the disuse of perfumes, oils and fine food; and the use of ashes, coarse food, and clothes. The time of mourning lasted from seven to 30 days and included outward expressions of sorrow for the dead and also signs of repentance.

Charles Zastrow writes in his book, *Understanding Human Behavior and the Social Environment*, "People in primitive societies handle death better than today's society."[5] They were more apt to view death as a natural occurrence, partly because they had a shorter life expectancy. They also frequently saw friends and relatives die. Because they viewed death as a natural occurrence, they were better prepared to handle the death of their loved ones.

In ancient Neanderthal burials, food, ornamental shells, and stone implements were buried with the dead, implying a belief that the dead would find such items useful during their passage from the land of the living to the dead. It is clear from evidence such as the Neanderthal burials that speculation about death and orderly practices for the grieving date from the earliest human societies.

Modern models and theories began with Sigmund Freud when he referred to emotions such as melancholia as mourning, meaning that one is searching for an attachment that has been lost. In the 1940s, Lindemann's work is considered a milestone of ideas about bereavement. His study was based on his intervention with 100 bereaved individuals, following the deaths of family and friends in a nightclub fire. From his study,

---

[5] Ibid.

Lindemann proposed six characteristics of acute grief.
Lindemann has provided a model and frame of reference that
allows for considering grief as work, with specific tasks to
accomplish.

Bowlby's Attachment Theory is another important
landmark in this field of study. In three volumes entitled
Attachment and Loss, he explores instinctive and attachment
behavior of humans and animals, the course of development
(ontogeny) of human attachment, an ethnological approach to
human fear, and the trauma of loss.

The most recognized historical landmark was a study
mentioned previously by Elisabeth Kubler-Ross that was
popular during the late 60's. Her landmark contribution, *On
Death and Dying*,[6] came at a time in the history of the United
States when stage approaches to psychological theorizing were
acceptable and death was a taboo subject. She opened the
doors to discussion and acknowledgement of death and to
addressing the loss experience.

Biblical

A Biblical image of grief is illustrated in several books,
which include Genesis, Numbers, Deuteronomy, and Job.
Grieving was expressed in many different ways by various
cultures from Genesis to Revelations. The book of Genesis
illustrates Abraham weeping and mourning when Sarah died
for it is natural to grieve over the loss of a beloved companion.
Genesis 23:2 states "And Sarah died in Kirjatharba; the same is

---

[6] Theresa A. Rando, *Grief, Dying and Death* (Chicago, Illinois: Research Press
Company 1969).

Hebron in the land of Canaan: and Abraham came to mourn for Sarah, and to weep for her." Abraham mourned and wept openly, which helps us to understand that grieving and mourning is natural.

Similarly, Jacob mourned at the loss of his son Joseph where comfort was initiated but Jacob refused. Genesis 37:34, 35 states "And Jacob rent his clothes, and put sackcloth upon his loins, and mourned for his son many days. And all his sons and all his daughters rose up to comfort him; but he refused to be comforted; and he said, for I will go down into the grave unto my son mourning. Thus his father wept for him."

This illustration reveals that the deep inner grief of a person may be shown outwardly. In Old Testament days, the torn garment and the wearing of the sackcloth were common signs of mourning. The loss of Jacob's son reveals to us that grief can be so intense that it almost can bring death to the mourner.

Jesus reminds us in Matthew 5:4 "blessed are they that mourn: for they shall be comforted." The greatest comforter, Jesus our Lord and Savior, wept at Lazarus' grave, which proves that all of us weep and mourn, and it is therefore all right to shed tears. Personally, I experienced mourning and comfort from God. Although the losses were painful, I contend that God was preparing me for the ultimate journey.

The most frequently and commonly used illustrations of grief are found in the book of Job. Job's experience with death is found nowhere else in the world. From the beginning of the book until its conclusion, we observe Job's challenge with his many encounters with grief. The book of Job presents a modern day story of life.

There are many people who are presently going through many of the trials seen in the Book of Job. Equally real are the attitudes and actions seen in Job's friends. Modern society always had those who desperately try to assist the grieving person and soon discover they are not equipped to give appropriate advice.

The Biblical text tells us of the servant Job, who was, "blameless and upright; he feared God and shunned evil."(Job 1:2 NIV). Job is described as a man who was respected among his peers, loved by his family, and financially stable. In today's language, he would be called the ideal man who "has it going on," but something disastrous happened. Without warning, Job's world began to crumble. I contend that Job's grief can best be described as compound or acute grief.

Theological

Many scholars and theologians question the grief Job suffered, but like Job, they have no right to question God's purpose. Furthermore, we must understand, as Jesus reminds us, that God's will was being done even through Job's grief. The mysteries and revelations of God often surface during our hour of grief and suffering. Theological questions are often raised concerning suffering and grief. The most commonly asked questions are: "if God loved me, why did this death occur?" "Could God have prevented it from happening?" Mourners ask: "where is God in our grief and suffering?" "Why does God permit grief and mourning?" I believe God does not want us to always ask or understand, but He wants us to trust, believe, and know that He is God!

During our grief and suffering, God arrests our attention, speaks to us, and gives specific instructions. The Lord spoke to the prophet Ezekiel and told him that his wife, the desire of his eyes, would succumb to a sudden death. Yet Ezekiel was not to mourn openly, but to remain silent (Ezekiel 24:15-24). Why did God ask Ezekiel to do something that seems so unfair, difficult, and unnatural? He wanted to illustrate to the people of Jerusalem that, just as the prophet's delight was taken from him, so also their delight, the temple, would be taken from them. God has a purpose. There is always a lesson from God. Therefore, we must acknowledge God in all things, understanding why He allows death, which results in grief and mourning. I believe God is involved in the life of all humanity through empathy.

The Apostle Paul reminds us in his letter to the Corinthian church of three specific prayers for physical healing that were never answered, "but he said to me, my grace is sufficient for you, for my power is made perfect in weakness.'" II Cor. 12:9 NIV I understand God saying, theologically, it's okay to be human, to suffer, and grieve.

Where was God when Jesus, God's only begotten Son, died on the cross? Could God have prevented that from happening? Does God suffer? Does God grieve? Jesus' death on the cross was not a result of loss, but in fact, was a result of love. John 3:16 states, "For God so loved the world, that he gave his only begotten Son..." Not all of God's creatures become attached through love. Mankind is the only creature that becomes attached through love. Mitchell and Anderson remind us "the work of grief can change our belief system about God." The principle theological question when confronted by loss and grief is not why we suffer, but who suffers with us? The affirmation that God suffers with us shifts our focus and belief. The question grief raises is not about God's power or goodness, but about God's faithfulness. Although I agree with this profound statement, the question remains—are we faithful to God?

In summary, humanity, through its limited knowledge, tries to understand God's purpose for our suffering through grief. I contend that our faith and trust in God is being tested through the process, which eventually helps build character. I am also reminded that when we take the Lord's Supper, we grieve for Christ's death. Moreover, as we celebrate the death of our risen Christ, we have hope that there is recovery from bereavement and grief. It is through Christ we can recover from any challenge.

Theological Reflection

Nehemiah, in the Old Testament reading, told the people not to mourn or weep about the law because God was showing His love for His people by giving them laws to help keep them safe. Nehemiah refers to the fact that God saw the people's afflictions under the Pharaoh of Egypt and opened the Red Sea for them.

There are a number of places in the Bible where people were given permission to grieve, to be sad, and to mourn over the loss of a loved one. As Jesus stated in the New Testament, "Blessed are they that mourn for they shall be comforted." Christians who believe that it is not appropriate to grieve need to hear and understand that message.

Because of my own grief experience, I believe that it is sometimes through mourning that we are able to find the peace and comfort God has for us. Therefore, we must learn that it is all right to grieve. We need to discover that grieving is good for us, mentally and spiritually, if processed properly.

When death invades our lives, our homes, and our hearts, often the question is asked, why is this happening to me? There are some who ask, "Where is God in this experience?" My theological reflection is that God is the same place He was when His only begotten son met death at the cross. I believe that God was rejoicing at that time. God, in His infinite wisdom, knew that through the death of His Son believers would have eternal life. God's will was being done on earth, and heaven could now rejoice. In fact, God surely grieved when His Son left home, but His grief was now over because His Son was back home.

Joan Guntzelman stated in her book "God knows you are grieving, do you know God is grieving. I have discovered through my personal grief experience that when we grieve God grieves with us. Isaiah 53:10 states, "yet it pleased the LORD to bruise him: he hath put him to grief: when thou shalt make his soul, an offering for sin, he shall see his seed, he shall prolong his days."[7]

I believe if we respond to God as Jesus would in the midst of death's pain, suffering, and afflictions, God will see us through. This allows us to understand that God responds to our grief. Finally, we will begin to see God as the Prophet Isaiah saw Him and we will understand that when someone dies, the vision becomes clearer. "In the year that king Uzziah died I saw also the Lord sitting upon a throne, high and lifted up, and his train filled the temple." (Isaiah 6:1 KJV).

---

[7] Guntzelman, God Knows You're Grieving.

CHAPTER TWO
What is grief?

There are several definitions of grief. According to research by Patrick Hill, "Grief is our reaction to loss; grief is a person's internal experience, thoughts and feelings related to the individual experience of a great loss. Grief is a normal process, an intense fundamental emotion, a universal experience which makes us human."[8]

In order to understand grief, we need to make the distinction between grief and bereavement/mourning. Grief leads to a state of bereavement or mourning. Bereavement and mourning are synonymous.

Bereavement disrupts physical functioning, manifesting such reactions as chills, diarrhea, fatigue, and profuse sweating. Emotional manifestations include intense and long-lasting reactions such as fear, anger, and sorrow. Bereavement affects cognitive functioning (e.g., memory distortions, attention deficits, and ongoing vigilance for danger) and behavior (e.g.,

---

[8] Patrick T. Hill and David Shirley, *A Good Death* (Reading, Massachusetts: Addison-Wesley, 1992).

sleep disturbances, excessive drinking, increased cigarette smoking, and reckless risk taking).[9]

Grief impacts social relationships as outsiders to the grief become noticeably uncomfortable when around the bereaved. More importantly, according to studies by David E. Balk, "grief and bereavement affects one's spirituality by challenging the griever's assumptions about the meaning of human existence."[10] Mourning is the external expression of one's grief. Thus, a person may experience extremely painful grief but because of a need to appear stoic, may not mourn.

Grief and bereavement are intensely personal and unique experiences. We often refer to stages of grief as noted by Kubler-Ross, which include denial, depression, anger, bargaining, and acceptance (see appendix A-J).[11] These often do not occur in an orderly progression. Depending on the situation or experience of the individual involved, one may not experience some stages, or may cycle in and out of the same emotional state several times. Here are the definitions of the five stages as noted by Kubler-Ross:.

Denial, numbness, and shock—This serves to protect the individual from experiencing the intensity of the loss. Numbness is a normal reaction to an immediate loss and should not be confused with "lack of caring." Denial and *disbelief

---

[9] "Trauma, Loss, & Bereavement"; http://www.selfgrowth.com/articles/Reece.html; Internet; (Accessed 03/04/2003 at 11:30 a.m.)

[10] D. E. Balk and N. S. Hogan, *Religion, Spirituality and Bereaved Adolescents* [Amityville, New York: Baywood Publications, 1995].

[11] Elisabeth Kubler-Ross, *On Death and Dying* [New York: The Macmillan Co., 1969].

will diminish as the individual slowly acknowledges the impact of this loss and the accompanying feelings.

Bargaining—At times, individuals may worry excessively about what could have been done to prevent the loss. Individuals can become preoccupied about ways that things could have been done better, imagining all the things that will never be. This reaction can provide insight into the impact of the loss; however, if not properly resolved, intense feelings of remorse and guilt may hinder the healing process.

Depression—After recognizing the true extent of the loss, some individuals may experience depressive symptoms. Sleep and appetite disturbance, lack of energy and concentration, and crying spells are some typical symptoms. Feelings of loneliness, emptiness, isolation, and self-pity can also surface during this phase, contributing to this reactive depression. For many, this phase must be experienced in order to begin reorganizing one's life.

Anger—This reaction usually occurs when an individual feels helpless and powerless. Anger may result from feeling abandoned, occurring in cases of loss through death. Feelings of resentment may occur toward oneself, a higher power, or toward life in general for the injustice of this loss. After an individual acknowledges anger, guilt may surface due to expressing these negative feelings. Again, these feelings are natural and should be honored to resolve the grief.

Acceptance—Time allows the individual an opportunity to resolve the range of feelings that surface. The grieving process supports the individual. That is, healing occurs when the loss becomes integrated into the individual's set of life experiences. Individuals may return to some of the earlier feelings throughout their life. There is no time limit to the grieving process. Each individual should define one's own healing process.

Pain and Suffering

A common denominator to all grief is some form of suffering. During the development of this project, I witnessed the emotional pain and suffering of several members from three separate congregations who experienced the loss of their Pastor through death. Several members from each congregation expressed a range of emotions that reflected the relationship each member had with their Pastor. The variations of emotions depended upon the length of the relationship established, the type of leadership provided to the member, and the type or style of ministry the pastor brought to the church.

There are several emotions associated with grief according to author Stephen Shuchter that include depression, anger, fear, acceptance, numbness, disbelief, shock, and emotional control. All emotions are forms of protection and shield individuals from reality. Although individuals experiencing grief may not display all of the symptoms[12] immediately, in time they will display one or more of them. The most common symptoms associated with grief include the following:

---

[12] Sharon L. Johnson, *Therapist Guide to Clinical Intervention: The 1-2-3's of Treatment Planning* (San Diego, California: Academic Press, 1979).

Symptoms of grief

✓ Anger
✓ Blaming yourself
✓ Crying spells
✓ Diarrhea
✓ Dizziness
✓ Fast heartbeat
✓ Feeling like there's a lump in your throat
✓ Feeling like what's happening around you isn't real
✓ Headaches
✓ Hyperventilating—sighing and yawning
✓ Nausea
✓ Not being able to get organized
✓ Not feeling hungry or losing weight
✓ Restlessness and irritability
✓ Sadness or depression
✓ Seeing images of the dead person
✓ Shortness of breath
✓ Tightness in your chest
✓ Tiredness
✓ Trouble concentrating
✓ Trouble sleeping

All of the symptoms mentioned can range from mild to severe. All of them are serious, and many of them often lead to some form of depression.

Depression

Depression is common in grief. Although not implied to be more severe than other symptoms listed, depression is usually the first stage experienced in grief according to Clayton, Halikas, and Maurice. Although depression symptoms vary from person to person, they include:
- Changes in sleep patterns
- Fatigue or lack of sleep
- Restlessness or slowed movements
- Trouble concentrating or making decisions

Depression is known as the single most common medical disorder encountered by widows and widowers.

I interviewed the widows of all three churches involved in the research study and discovered all of them experienced depression accompanied by various symptoms of grief such as mood swings, loss of appetite, crying spells, trouble sleeping and anger. I also discovered somatic symptoms including hopelessness and worthlessness.

According to Clayton in his 1990 research, more than half of all widowed participants had crying spells, sleep disturbances, low mood, loss of appetite, fatigue, and/or poor memory at some time during the first year of bereavement. In general, somatic symptoms gradually improve, whereas psychological symptoms (e.g., hopelessness) persist.

A further study conducted by Blanchard, Blanchard and Becker, also found that somatic symptoms decrease by the end of the first year but that a depressed mood, restlessness, hopelessness, worthlessness, and suicidal thoughts did not subside during that same time frame.

I discovered various similar symptoms of depression from candidates who were interviewed from the three churches who lost their Pastor to death. The symptoms included mood swings, loss of appetite, insomnia, and anger.[13] The members who received little or no grief intervention, such as counseling or follow-up workshops, experienced a great deal of suffering. As a result, research revealed that 80% of the workshop participants suffered from unresolved grief.

Common myths about grief

- Children grieve like adults
- Grief is the same after all types of death
- It takes two months to get over your grief
- All bereaved people grieve in the same way
- Your grief will decline over time without any upsurges
- When grief is resolved, it never comes up again
- You and your family will be the same after the death of a loved one
- It is not okay to feel sorry for yourself
- There is no reason to be angry at your deceased loved one
- Men and women grieve in the same ways
- Children need to be protected from grief and death
- You will have no relationship with your loved one after his or her death

---

[13] Stephen R. Shuchter *Dimensions of Grief* (San Francisco, California: Jossey-Bass, 1986).

- Parents usually divorce after a child dies
- Once your loved one has died, it is better not to focus on him or her but to put him or her in the past and go on with your life.

These and other myths can make the process of grieving more painful and difficult by creating unrealistic expectations for your recovery and preventing the griever from seeking the support needed.[14]

---

[14] Therese A. Rando, *Grief, Dying and Death* (Chicago, Illinois: Research Press, 1984).

CHAPTER THREE
How to grieve

There is no correct or incorrect way to grieve. Grief is a journey, a process that takes time and hard emotional work. It is an individual experience. No one mourns the same way. Some may feel worse early on, and some may feel worse months, even years, later. Some experience grief unpredictably—feeling "fine" one minute and in pain another.

Many want to talk about what they are going through; others seem to want to deal with their feelings on their own. The next ten suggestions on how to grieve may help educate the griever, as well as assist them during the grieving process:

1. **Feel your feelings fully.** Grievers may experience many feelings such as deep sadness, depression, loneliness, guilt, anger, anguish, confusion, relief, and emptiness. Whatever the experience, they seem to judge the feeling. Stephen Levine, author and teacher, calls grief "the pain that ends the pain." Use your emotions to help you heal and to eventually help you live without the person who has now gone. Surrender to your body's wisdom. If you need to cry, cry. If you need to really wail, do that too. If you need to pound on a pillow or walk and run until you feel exhausted, go right ahead. The body will respond to

the emotion that is felt if the griever will just give in and not be afraid to feel fully and deeply.

2. **Be patient with your body's physical experiences during grief.** The griever may not be able to sleep well or may sleep a lot. Some people use food to comfort themselves and eat too much or eat inappropriately while others cannot eat at all. Some people have waves of anxiety wash over them which leave them feeling nervous or dizzy, some will feel tightness in their chest and feel like they cannot get a deep breath, some tremble, others feel sick to their stomachs, and some feel dry mouthed. These are just some reactions to anxiety. Many people feel listless and unable to concentrate. Some distract themselves with frenetic activity as a way to get away from the feelings. Some people just feel like they are "going crazy." All of this is a normal reaction to grief. The emotional and physical feelings sometimes last a long time, but for others it is relatively brief.

3. **Give yourself time to grieve.** Grief will last as long as it lasts. Many people think they are failing at healing if they cannot seem to reach closure after a certain period of time. They have an expectation of when they should feel better and that expectation can make healing an added burden. There is no simple answer to how long grief lasts. So many variables make no one answer acceptable. Each griever and each situation of loss is unique. Some of the variables include the personality of the griever, whether or not loss has been experienced before, the nature and quality of the relationship before the loss, their own coping mechanisms and support

systems, whether the loss was expected or sudden, and whether they feel responsible in some way for that loss.

4. **Remember grief is a process and may be a lifelong endeavor.** Some grief takes much longer, and sometimes it is never really over. A part of us may feel like we will never get over our loss and yet, at the same time, we need to find meaningful ways to live life in new ways and let go of what was. Otherwise, grief takes over, we feel stuck, and our lives become stagnated.

5. **Find ways to honor your grief.** Allow grief its time. Talk about your feelings or use a journal to record your thoughts and feelings. Do not push yourself to resume all your activities right away. Do not try to replace the loss or the emptiness with activities, people, or things; what is lost is not replaceable. Our daily routines and structure can help us move on without them and adjust to the changes brought about in their absence and the grief that follows.

6. **Find ways to honor your loved one.** Celebrate your memories. Create a story, a poem, or song about the person you cared about who is now gone. Locate photos or other memorabilia that can be collected in a book or special container for safekeeping. Some use candles and fresh flowers as a way to honor the one who has died. Others use a hobby, such as gardening, sewing, woodworking, or creative art expression, as a way to create a memorial in honor of the one who is no longer present. All of these are suggestions to help bring comfort as you work through grief and help recognize that the person is still in your memories.

7. **Get help if your grief seems unrelenting and you seem unable to let go.** In order to cope with the pain of grief, some use drugs or alcohol to ease or numb the pain. Usually this only distorts and/or prolongs the grief and can develop into other problems. Consider a support group, a counselor, or clergyperson to talk with. There are excellent books on death, and dying, and grieving that are enormously helpful because they let us know we are not alone and will often validate our experiences. As mentioned earlier, grief can last months, even years, but if it takes up most of our energy, is still a primary focus, and we are unable to function well, then the grief may be stagnated and thus our lives are stagnated. Also note, if the feeling and symptoms of grief are still quite acute after a year or so, that may be an indication that you need to seek help.

8. **Expect anniversary reactions.** This is not stagnated grief. Special times of the year, such as holidays, birthdays, or the anniversary of the death or divorce, may bring up a flood of feelings for a time. This is normal. Sometimes the flood of feelings comes at odd times. Emotions just wash over you and it may help to do something to honor the person in some way on that occasion.

9. **Use grief to assess the way you live.** Let grief remind you of the preciousness of life and how precarious it can be. In the blink of an eye, all can change. Live with yourself and with others with this in mind.

10. **Let your grief call you to a new way of living.** Letting go of past hurts, forgiving, living life fully each day, and

not taking anyone or anything for granted are some possibilities for beginning anew with a sense of the gift of life. Let grief teach about the meaning of life and love. It can be a difficult teacher and quite a wise one.[15]

---

[15] www.brandywinepastoral.org/body-publhtml; Internet; Accessd on 8/26/2003 at 3:00 a.m.

"If we allow ourselves to grieve, it liberates us..."

CHAPTER FOUR
The Benefits of Grief

There are several benefits for the griever who must yield to grief in order to effectively begin the healing process. The first benefit of grief is that it allows us to be honest with ourselves and honest with God. If we allow ourselves to grieve, it liberates us to the point where we can be open to disclose and express our feelings overall. Thus it allows us to view ourselves as God views us.

Personal growth often comes out of loss. Many participants stated that, after their experience, they had growth in areas they would not have grown in otherwise. Better understanding of one's self is a common result for those who experienced grief. The three most important aspects are understanding their strengths, their weaknesses, and their limitations.

Another important benefit of grief is remaining healthy during the process. When we are able to grieve properly, we are less susceptible to physical ailments and complications to current diseases/ailments/conditions. For example, if a griever suffers from asthma during time of grief, asthma attacks may become more acute and more frequent. If the griever has an ailment that is severe, such as cancer, the griever may not want to live anymore because their loved one is no longer there.

Educational opportunities are a valuable benefit for many experiencing grief and bereavement. The griever learns from experience what grievers and supporters should and should not be doing during this critical hour. The story was recorded of a deacon at Gath Baptist Church in McMinnville, Tennessee whose wife died of incurable liver cancer. The deacon received comfort and compassion up to and during the funeral. Immediately after the funeral, however, the phone calls and visits stopped. The deacon was hurt and angered by what he considered a lack of concern, but has since learned that it was not intentional.

He began to read books on death and the grieving process. In addition to learning where he was in the process, he began to get a better understanding "of what people should be doing but were afraid to do." Instead of letting his anger drive him to leave the church and never tell anyone why, the deacon addressed the deacon board three weeks after his wife's death, and told them his concerns, and how he felt about their lack of response. They were upset that they had not done anything, the deacon discovered. He also realized that he had gone too far with the deacons and later apologized. In additional reading, he learned that it would have been appropriate for him to call friends and tell them that he needed someone to talk to.

The main thing he discovered about the participants of the Pleasant Grove Baptist Church is that they all "needed the presence of someone, someone to talk to, someone to share feelings with, and not be uncomfortable with."

I discovered that what happened was not a unique situation, but is symptomatic of churches of all denominations. People just do not know what to do or say. People want to get involved, but they are afraid they will say the wrong thing. This leads to the next benefit, which is the development of ministry.

As a result of crisis and education, the deacons of Gath church began to discuss what they could do in terms of ministry to others who would face crisis. The grief-stricken deacon stepped in to do his part to see that no one else in the church would have to go through a similar experience.

The participants of the Pleasant Grove Church after the third workshop, discussed what they could do in terms of ministry. As a result, the grief and bereavement ministry was developed. One member stated, "unless we make an attempt to get involved with them in their grief, there is a good possibility they will fall by the wayside, and we will not know why they left the church."

I began to reflect upon his own personal experience of how grief was dealt with in the past and to compare it to how he I dealt with the recent death of his my son. Using a different approach and responding effectively can make all the difference in the world. As an unbeliever, my response was self-help and self-medication. However, as a believer in Christ, the grief allowed me to draw closer to God and the testimony of His written Word, increasing my faith and trust in God. For the believer, this is one of the greatest benefits of grief.

I reflected on how David was able to resolve his feelings of grief through the knowledge of the salvation of his child and return to the house of worship. After David's child was struck by the Lord, he became ill. David fasted and prayed for many days and nights. According to 2 Samuel 12:15-23 "After the child died, David got up from the ground, washed, and anointed himself; he went into the house of the LORD and worshipped. When asked why are you acting this way David replied, "can I bring him back again? I will go to him, but he will not return to me."[16]

Further reflection reveals that Jesus recognized mourning and grief as valid emotions, but grief is always accompanied by a commensurate joy. John 16:20 states "I tell you the truth, you will weep and mourn while the world rejoices. You will grieve, but your grief will turn into joy." What a comforting affirmation.

Finally, it is the believer's faith in God and the hope of heaven that helps us deal with grief, as the Apostle Paul reminds us in 1Thessalonians 4:13-14: "Brothers, we do not want you to be ignorant about those who fall asleep, or to grieve like the rest of men, who have no hope. We believe that Jesus died and rose again and so we believe that God will bring with Jesus those who have fallen asleep in him."

---

[16] 2 Samuel 12:20-23; All Scripture references are taken from the King James Version unless otherwise noted.

CHAPTER FIVE
Pastoral Care and Counseling
Counsel in the heart of man is like deep water, but a man of understanding will draw it out. Proverbs 20:5 KJV

There is a tremendous need for pastoral care and counselors in the areas concerning grief. Offering effective and non-judgmental pastoral care to the bereaved is a task for a pastor who possesses the skills of a professional counselor. There is a great danger with those who seek help from anyone other than a professional. Counseling from a licensed professional, such as a counselor or chaplain, can provide and stimulate growth and development to help the bereaved cope more effectively with the loss.

The counselor or Chaplain who follows the example of Jesus must show compassion, mercy, and love, while facilitating effective non-judgmental pastoral care. The counselor or chaplain must also provide unconditional love and offer care that is sensitive to the needs of the grieved.

Additionally, the counselor or chaplain can provide prayer and comforting Scriptures, as well as help increase the faith of the individual. The Counselor or Chaplain should also refer the grieved to a professional physician or psychiatrist or have one on staff who can provide the medical attention needed for the individual.

Moreover, The counselor can provide the proper diagnosis, implement treatment plans, and provide additional therapy that will help make some adjustments and stabilize the griever's thought processes, if needed. Moreover, the counselor can help facilitate the griever through the grief process.

Finally, the best skill a counselor possesses to assist a grieving member is the ability to listen. More than 50% of the participants interviewed stated that "they wanted the opportunity to talk, share, express, cry, and have someone who would just listen and care." They did not necessarily want a response, just an ear.

The Role of the Holy Spirit
"Blessed are they who that mourn, for they shall be comforted."
(Matthew 5:4) (KJV)

The Holy Spirit's role in the life of the believer has many functions. The role of comforting our spirit is the one a believer depends on when experiencing grief. The Holy Spirit is the Comforter, which in Greek is called *Parakletos*, meaning intercessor, counselor, advocate, and comforter. The verb *paraklysis* means solace, comfort, consolation, exhortation, and entreaty which refer to God comforting us in our distress and mourning.

The participants of the workshops, all believers in Christ, expressed that there is a greater spiritual healing and comfort that comes from the Holy Spirit. Also, for many, it is the Holy Spirit that leads and guides them through their grief experience. However, three workshop participants who were raised in the church expressed that during their grief experience their religion and faith were shattered. Subsequently, this delayed the acceptance of the loss of their pastor.

The believer calls on their Christian experience that assures them that God through the Holy Spirit will provide spiritual and emotional support to assist them through their grief process. Subsequently, the believer uses Scripture as a textbook testifying to what God has done for others such as healing and deliverance. As one believer stated, "it is in the (Bible) textbook that we, the believers, will find refuge, peace, assurance, and comfort." Furthermore, the believer uses prayer as a form of communication to God through the Holy Spirit, which gives them a sense of peace, assurance, and comfort.

1 Thessalonians 4:13 helps the believers affirm their faith for it states, "we need not grieve as those who have no hope." Since we have hope and God's presence, we are freed to grieve deeply, to experience our losses. As a believer and griever, it is our relationship with God and our faith that prepares us to grieve deeply.

Jesus said, "And I will pray the Father and he shall give you another Comforter, that he may abide with you for ever."[17] The Holy Spirit does comfort and console us in our loss, if we avail ourselves of this experience.

Unresolved or Unsuccessful Grief

Unresolved grief is common in today's society, as it was in ages past. When grief is unresolved, it can lead to denial,

---

[17]John 14:16

anger, bargaining, acute anxiety, and depression.
Unfortunately, unresolved grief can affect a person's physical,
emotional, mental, social, spiritual, and psychological
behavior. Avoidance is a common denominator as it relates to
unresolved grief.

In a recent study for psychological intervention
concluded by Edward J. Callahan, Ph.D. reveals that

. . . human grieving can be understood by
considering behavior associated with
traumatic aversive events. Classically
conditioned stimuli associated with the
deceased were once predominantly positive,
but may now provoke uncomfortable
physiological, behavioral, and cognitive
change as known conditioned emotional
responses (CERs).

Continued exposure to CERs results in a
diminution of the disruptive power of these
stimuli. Avoidance of the stimuli leaves the
disruptive power stimulus intact; this
disruption can even increase over time.
Those who experience loss that is out of the
normal developmental sequence and those
who learn avoidance as a primary coping
technique may be particularly vulnerable to
unresolved grief.

Individuals who cope using avoidance
may fail to experience and hence work
through their loss. Under such
circumstances, a pronounced focus on bodily
symptoms may occur, making presentation to

primary care a possible course for unresolved grief.[18]

There are several treatments and interventions available for unresolved grief such as medication and counseling. According to R.W. Ramsey a noted counselor:

... the basic rationale for treatment of unresolved grief is similar to that of the rationale for flooding procedures. Flooding involves prolonged exposure to intense stimuli which had been avoided. Through exposure, these stimuli lose their power and adaptive functioning returns.

Flooding is a corrective procedure used when excessive avoidance and escape prevents the griever from prolonged exposure to the feared stimuli, thus maintaining disruption of behavior. Flooding requires moderated presentation of aversive events with gradually increasing exposure. Moderation maintains the cooperation of the patient.[19]

A therapeutic rationale to enlist the patient is a key part of the treatment plan: "Wounds fail to heal if not adequately cleaned and exposed to air. If you continue with that wound

---

[18] "Psychological Intervention for unresolved Grief"; Available at www.ncptsd.org/publications/ cq/v5/n2-3/callahan.html; Internet; Accessed 9/30/2003 at 3:00 a.m.

[19] R. W. Ramsey, *Bereavement: A behavioral treatment of pathological grief* (New York: Academic Press, 1979).

unexposed and avoid the cleaning process, the wound can deepen and fester. With unresolved grief it is important to open the wound by exposure to many reminders of the loss. This painful exposure will lead step by step to thorough and healthy healing."

Critical to this therapeutic rationale is that it counters accepted theory about loss. The Freudian notion was "that one had to end attachment to the person who died in order to make a successful adjustment to life." "An alternate rationale is to attach to the deceased so they no longer need to be avoided: Saying hello again rather than saying good bye. Through discussion the therapist helps the griever recall what was special about the lost relationship so that the loss can be more fully appreciated. Discussion of the relationship facilitates exposure to stimulus associated with the loss" according to Marvin White.[20]

Further therapeutic research reveals patients with unresolved grief may have suicidal ideation or plans. These need to be determined early in the therapeutic relationship to ensure development of a safe environment for flooding. A written contract may not be needed, but it is important to obtain at least verbal agreement that the patient will not hurt him or herself without first calling the therapist. Thus, the therapist must be available to the patient in a controlled fashion should a crisis arise. The patient can agree to write out antecedents and potential coping efforts whenever a suicidal thought arises as a bridging step in this process aimed toward greater patient self-control. Patients can use this process to

---

[20] Marvin White, "Saying Hello Again: The incorporation of the lost relationship in the resolution of grief," *Dulwich Centre Newsletter*, Adelaide, South Australia.

increase their understanding of their urges to hurt themselves and to decrease the need to call the therapist. Contacting and writing can serve as therapeutic tools for fighting against avoidance.

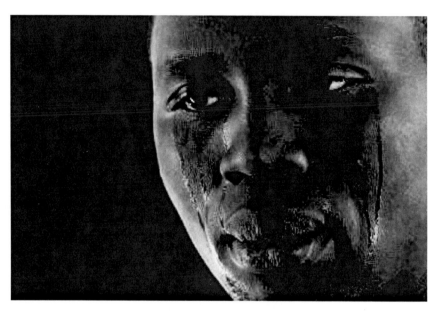

*"Having the courage to confront death inevitably means
that we examine our lives, our values, our ideas,
our sense of meaning and more importantly, our faith."*

CHAPTER SIX
Resolving Grief and Bereavement
The 5F Formula

The problem many 21st century grievers struggle with is that they do not know how to cope with grief or effectively process it. In order to effectively cope with, process, and resolve grief, three interventions are necessary:. First, a professional counselor to help with the psychological and emotional aspects of grief. Secondly, a spiritual leader to promote spiritual stability. Lastly, resources which give the griever options to explore.

Kubler-Ross' final phase of the process in dealing with loss is acceptance. The final goal for the griever to achieving resolution is acceptance. There are several important components needed to effectively process grief after acceptance is achieved. I have therefore developed a five-step process, which I call the 5F process. The 5F process includes facing, feeling, fueling, freeing, and faith in the grief. The methods should be facilitated in a group session or individual sessions by a licensed professional, such as a counselor or chaplain. The 5F process is as follows:

1. **Grievers need to *face* the grief:**

The griever needs to recognize their responsibility and respond with action. The individual griever can face their grief through courage, emotional maturity, and faith. When we face grief, we must have the courage and willingness to accept, acknowledge, and cope with the reality of the grief. Judy Tatelbaum states, "acknowledgement can be the antidote to denial and secondly, courage is one the greatest assets we can possess for facing life and death."[21]

Having the courage to confront death inevitably means that we examine our lives, our values, our ideas, our sense of meaning, and more importantly, our faith. As a direct result, we will begin to re-examine our purpose for living through the experience. Subsequently, this leads us to trust and have faith in God. Then, facing grief becomes easier.

2. Grievers need to *feel* the grief:

Feeling the pain of grief is therapeutic. Expressing and sharing of feelings are important. Grievers need to know the importance of this expression of feelings and how therapeutic it is. Feeling leads to healing. It is rare that only one or a few emotions are present. In fact, they are multiple and vary with time. Tears and crying are the first feelings expressed during this period. Depression and thoughts of suicide are common. Feelings of abandonment, loneliness, sexual dysfunctions of various kinds, and guilt are common. Joan Guntzelman states "unexpressed emotions do not disappear, they go underground and resurface and affect us in other ways. We miss the wisdom

---

[21] Judy Tatelbaum *The Courage to Grieve* (New York: Lippincott & Crowell Publishers, Inc., 1980).

of our emotions the healing the can bring to our experience."[22]
Therefore, grievers need to feel what is present, take the time
to be aware of what they are feeling, and express it. This allows
healing to begin.

3. Grievers need to *fuel* the grief:

Fuel burns and allows the process to move forward. We
must allow the fuel of grief to burn our innermost feelings, to
cleanse us of the hurt and pain. Fueling is the purifier. The grief
can be fueled by a professional grief counselor and support
groups, including family members. With proper ventilation and
facilitation, this process will allow the griever to express all of
their feelings and will provide the capacity to cope with them
as they are disclosed.

We often deny our ambivalent feelings and idealize the
loved one instead. We remember just the good things and deny
that we had bad experiences with the loved one. (This was the
case with the church and the death of the pastor; no one talked
about negative or bad experiences). There comes a time when
every griever should unload every emotion that they are
feeling. The expression of all of one's emotions is important
because it cleanses the spirit and body of the griever.

There are many who grieve over someone they did not
like. Feelings of hate and resentment are suppressed when they
should be disclosed. John James states in *The Grief Recovery
Handbook* that "truth is the key to recovery. The essence of
recovery is contained in the premise of being totally honest

---

[22] Joan Guntzelman, *God knows Your Grieving* (Notre Dame, Indiana: Sorin
Books, 2001).

about ourselves in relation to others."[23] Many times, these feelings are never expressed. They must be fueled in order for the healing process to begin.

The griever needs to pour out their heart to God. Tell God exactly how they feel. It is okay to get angry with God. Job expressed his feelings, pain, and suffering in Job 7:11. He states: "Therefore I will not refrain restrain my mouth; I will speak in the anguish of my spirit; I will complain in the bitterness of my soul." God blessed Job for speaking his mind. After we talk it over with God, then we are prepared to free the grief.

4. Grievers need to *free* the grief:

The griever starts to surrender to reality. They need to begin the process of letting go of the grief, facing reality, and moving on. One important goal in grief, according to John Naperkoski "is for the survivor to transfer the deceased from the place of reality they formerly occupied in their life to one of memory."[24] This final stage is critical for recovery. The healing has begun at this stage.

5. Grievers now have the *faith* to know that recovery is a reality:

Where is your faith? Allow your faith to lead you. Allow your faith to grow. The focus is not death but life. It is time to process a more structured, organized, healthy, active, social, hard working, positive, and purposeful life. Though I said it

[23] John James and Russell Friedman, *The Grief Recovery Handbook* (New York: Harper Collins Publishers Inc., 1998).

[24] Ibid., 15.

earlier, it bears repeating. Faith dictates the outcome of God's grace. When we exercise our faith God will complete the process.

It's time to move from grief to God's grace!

BIBLIOGRAPHY

Balk, D. E., and N. S. Hogan. *Religion, Spirituality and Bereaved Adolescents.* Amityville, New York: Baywood Publications, 1995.

Churn, Arlene. *The End is Just the Beginning: Lessons in Grieving for African Americans.* New York: Random House Inc., 2003.

Coleman, Penny. *Corpses, Coffins, and Crypts.* New York: Henry Holt and Company, 1997.

Creswell, John W. *Research and Design Qualitative and Quantitative and Mixed Method Approaches.* 2nd edition. Thousand Oaks, California: Sage Publications, Inc., 2003.

Dunn, Michael. *The Good Grief Guide: How to Come Through Bereavement with Hope for the Future and at Peace with the Past.* Oxford, United Kingdom: How to Books Ltd., 2000.

DeHaan, Dennis J. *Our Daily Bread.* Grand Rapids, Michigan: RBC Ministries, 2002.

Despelder, Lynn Ann, and Albert Lee Strickland. *The Last Dance: Encountering Death and Dying.* 4th edition.

Mountain View, California: Mayfield Publishing Company, 1995.

Fowler, James W. *Stages of Faith: The psychology of human development and the quest for meaning*. San Francisco, California: Harper and Row, 1981.

Freud, Sigmund. *Mourning and Melancholia in R. V. Frankiel*. New York: University Press, 1994.

Guntzelman, Joan. *God Knows You're Grieving*. Notre Dame, Indiana: Sorin Books, 2001.

Hill, Patrick T., and David Shirley. *A Good Death*. Reading, Massachusetts: Addison-Wesley, 1992.

Hospice Foundation of America. *Living With Grief: Who We Are, How We Grieve*. Washington, DC: HFA Publications, 1998.

Hughes, Marylou. *Bereavement and Support: Healing in a Group Environment*. New York: Taylor & Francis Group, 1995.

Hunter, George I. *Supervision and Education-Formation for Ministry*. Cambridge, Massachusetts: Episcopal Divinity School, 1982.

James, John W. and Russell Friedman. *The Grief Recovery Handbook*. New York: Harper-Collins Publishers Inc., 1998.

Johnson, Sharon L. *Therapist Guide to Clinical Intervention The 1-2-3's of Treatment Planning*. San Diego, California: Academic Press, 1979.

Kubler-Ross, Elisabeth. *On Death and Dying*. New York: The Macmillin Co., 1969.

Mitchell, K. and H. Anderson. *All Our Losses, All Our Griefs*. Philadelphia, Pennsylvania: The Westminster Press, 1993.

Nouwen, Henri J. *The Wounded Healer*. New York, Doubleday, 1979.

Pohly, Kenneth. *Transforming The Rough Places: The Ministry of Supervision*. Dayton, OH: Whaleprints, 1993.

Ramsey, R. W. *Bereavement: A Behavior Treatment Of Pathological Grief*. New York: Academic Press, 1979.

Rando, Therese A. *Grief, Dying, and Death*. Chicago, Illinois: Research Press Company, 1984.

Rasberry, Salli and Carole Rae Watanabe. *The Art of Dying*. Berkeley, California: Celestial Arts, 1995.

Sanders, Catherine M. *Grief the Mourning After*. 2nd edition. New York: John Wiley & Sons, Inc., 1999.

Shuchter, Stephen R. *Dimensions of Grief*. San Francisco, California: Jossey-Bass, Inc. Publishers, 1986.

Staudacher, Carol. *Men and Grief*. Oakland, California: New Harbinger Publications, 1991.

Tatelbaum, Judy. *The Courage to Grieve: Creative Living Recovery & Growth through Grief*. New York: Lippincott & Crowell Publishers, Inc., 1980.

Westberg, Granger E. *Good Grief*. Philadelphia, Pennsylvania: Fortress Press, 1971.

White, Marvin *Saying Hello Again: The incorporation of the lost relationship in the resolution of grief*. Adelaide, South Australia: Dulwich Centre Newsletter.

www.brandywinepastoral.org/body-publ.html

www.ncptsd.org/publications/cq/v5/n2-3/callahan.html.9/29/2003.4:00am

www.selfgrowth.com/articles/reece.html.03/04/2003.11#0am

Zastrow, Charles and Karen K. Kirstk-Ashman. *Understanding Human Behavior and the Social Environment*. Chicago, Illinois: Nelson Hall Publishing, 1995.

APPENDIX A
LEARNING HISTORY

1. What did you learn from your family that you have carried on in how you interact with people, the community (POSITIVE AND NEGATIVE)?

_____

_____

_____

2. How do you deal with your emotions?

_____

_____

_____

3. How do you deal with anger?

_____

_____

_____

4. How would you rate your self-esteem?

_____

_____

_____

5. How do you take care of yourself?

_____

_____

_____

6. What are the consequences of your behaviors?

_____

_____

_____

7. What are your choices?

_____

_____

_____

8. What changes do you need to continue working on in order to reach your goals?

_____

_____

_____

APPENDIX B
HOW DO YOU KNOW YOU ARE READY?

YOU KNOW YOU ARE READY WHEN:
1. You have acknowledged that a problem exists.
2. You have acknowledged that the problem is associated with the loss.
3. You acknowledged that you are now willing to deal with your loss.

FINDING THE SOLUTION:
THE FIVE STAGES OF RECOVERING LOSS:
1. Growing Awareness-that issues are unresolved
2. Accepting Responsibility-for resolving the loss
3. Identifying-what you need to do to resolve the loss
4. Taking action-to resolve the loss
5. Moving beyond Loss-through sharing with others and taking action which facilitates resolution and growth.

HOW DO YOU DEAL WITH LOSS?
People deal with loss in various ways. Do you identify with any of the following examples?
1. Intellectualize-don't deal with feelings, don't talk or write about how they feel
2. Be fine and put on a happy face for those around you "Academy Award Winning Recovery."

3. Want the approval of others; want others to be accepting of your feelings.

4. Acting out ("don't expect anything of me because I hurt so badly")

OTHER WAYS?

Write about how you have dealt with the loss(es) you have experienced, and be prepared to discuss it.

APPENDIX C
SCRIPTURES OF COMFORT

Isaiah 66:13 – As one whom his mother comforteth, so will I comfort you; and ye shall be comforted in Jerusalem.

2 Corinthians 1:3 – Blessed *be* God, even the Father our Lord Jesus Christ, the Father of mercies, and the God of all comfort.

Matthew 9:22 – But Jesus turned him about, and when he saw her, he said, Daughter, be of good comfort; thy faith hath made thee whole. And the woman was made whole from that hour.

Luke 7:13 – And when the Lord saw her, he had compassion on her, and said unto her, Weep not.

John 14:1 – Let not your heart be troubled: ye believe God, believe also in me.

John 14:18 – I will not leave you comfortless: I will come to you.

John 16:33 – These things I have spoken unto you, that in me ye might have peace. In the world ye shall have tribulation: but be of good cheer; I have overcome the world.

Isaiah 40:1 – Comfort ye, comfort ye my people, saith your God.

1 Corinthians 14:31 – For ye may all prophesy one by one, that all may learn, and all may be comforted.

2 Corinthians 2:7 – So that contrariwise ye *ought* rather to forgive *him*, and comfort *him*, lest perhaps such a one should be swallowed up with overmuch sorrow.

1 Thessalonians 5:11 – Wherefore comfort yourselves together, and edify one another, even as also ye do.

1 Thessalonians 5:14 – Now we exhort you, brethren, warm them that are unruly, comfort the feebleminded, support the weak, be patient toward all *men*.

APPENDIX D
SIMPLE SOLUTIONS

There are many more simple solutions that can assist the griever in their process. Listed below are twenty-five suggestions made by Marylou Hughes from her book *Bereavement and Support: Healing in a Group Environment* that can help people through their grief experience.

1. Be patient with yourself. Do not compare yourself to others. Go through the mourning process at your own pace.

2. Admit you are hurting and go with the pain.

3. Apply cold or heat to your body, whichever feels best.

4. Ask for and accept help.

5. Talk to others.

6. Face the loss.

7. Stop asking, "Why?" Instead ask, "What will I do now?"

8. Recognize that a bad day does not mean that all is lost.

9. Rest.

10. Exercise.

11. Keep to a routine.

12. Introduce pleasant changes into your life.

13. Know that you will survive.

14. Take care of something alive, such as a plant or a pet.

15. Schedule activities to help you get through weekends and holidays.

16. Find someone who needs your help.

17. Accept your feelings as part of the normal grief reaction.

18. Postpone major decisions whenever possible.

19. Do something you enjoy doing.

20. Write in a journal.

21. Be around people.

22. Schedule time alone.

23. Do not overdo.

24. Eat regularly.

25. Pray and meditate.[25]

---

[25] http://www.survivingsuicide.com/grief.htm; Internet; Accessed 9/30/2003 at 4:00 a.m.

My 5F Grief Journal
Journaling God's Grace to Me
*How Am I **Facing** My Grief?*

_____

_____

_____

_____

_____

_____

_____

_____

_____

_____

_____

_____

_____

_____

_____

_____

_____

_____

_____

_____

_____

_____

_____

_____

_____

_____

_____

_____

_____

_____

_____

_____

_____

_____

_____

_____

Journaling God's Grace to Me
*How Am I **Feeling** My Grief?*

_____

_____

_____

_____

_____

_____

_____

_____

_____

_____

_____

_____

_____

_____

_____

_____

_____

_____

Journaling God's Grace to Me
*How Am I **Fueling** My Grief?*

_____

_____

_____

_____

_____

_____

_____

_____

_____

_____

_____

_____

_____

_____

_____

_____

_____

_____

_____

_____

_____

_____

_____

_____

_____

_____

_____

_____

_____

_____

_____

_____

_____

_____

_____

_____

_____

_____

_____

_____

_____

_____

_____

Journaling God's Grace to Me
*How Am I **Freeing** My Grief?*

_____

_____

_____

_____

_____

_____

_____

_____

_____

_____

_____

_____

_____

_____

_____

_____

_____

_____

_____

_____

_____

_____

_____

_____

_____

_____

_____

_____

_____

_____

_____

_____

_____

_____

_____

_____

_____

_____

_____

_____

Journaling God's Grace to Me
*How Am I Showing **Faith** Through My Grief?*

_____

_____

_____

_____

_____

_____

_____

_____

_____

_____

_____

_____

_____

_____

_____

_____

_____

About the Author

The joy of the Lord always shines upon the face of Reverend Dr. Edward Robert Knox. It is the fruit of the Spirit that God graced Edward with that draws people to Christ through him. There is joy in his singing, joy in his preaching, joy in his praise, and there is joy in his spirit. Reverend Knox proclaims, "The Joy of the Lord is my strength." Nehemiah 8:10

Raised in Detroit Michigan as a child he was educated in the Detroit Public Schools. A lover of music and avid sports fan Edward loved to play baseball and sing in the choir while attending Martin Luther King High School.

Baptized at the age of nine Edward knew the Lord had a calling upon his life. His joy was attending church. In 1983 Woodward Avenue Presbyterian Church and served as Chairman of the Deacon Board and thus began to grow spiritually. He ultimately accepted the call to the ministry in 1991, and was ordained in 1999 by his Pastor, and mentor Reverend Dr. Joseph R. Jordan. Edward's ministry began to grow as he taught Old Testament classes for MEDCCE. He also served as Chaplain for United Health Services.

His academic journey began at The Southern Baptist Theological Seminary School where he received a diploma in Pastoral Ministries. Edward continued his academic pursuit and in 1998 he graduated from Spring Arbor University in with a Bachelor of Arts degree in Family Life Education and was selected the class president. Subsequently, he continued his education and in 2001 he graduated from Ashland Theological

Seminary with a Master of Arts in Pastor Counseling. He earned his Doctorate of Ministry Degree in Counseling and Pastoral Care from United Theological Seminary in the fall of 2003.

Dr. Reverend Edward Knox aggregate community service was extensive. In 1998 he helped implement a state wide HIV/AIDS Program where he eventually served as the Executive Director of the Southern Christian Leadership Conference. He continued to serve the community and helped implement the Safe Streets Program with the National Conference for Community and Justice. He also hosted a radio program on WDTR for two years entitled Point of Action. In 2004, then Governor Jennifer Granholm appointed him to serve on the State Board of Chiropractors. He also serves as a Board member for the Southern Christian Leadership Conference Detroit Chapter. Dr. Knox is featured in the national magazine 2010 edition of the *Who's Who Leading Ministers in Detroit*.

Reverend Knox served as the youth Pastor at Corinthian Baptist Church in 2000 under the leadership of Pastor Jordan. He later served as the assistant Pastor at Metropolitan Baptist Church under the leadership of Dr. Jerome Washington. Dr. Knox is currently the Pastor of The New Mt. Vernon Baptist Church in Detroit. He served as the Chairman of the Education Committee for The Council of Baptist Pastors of Detroit and Vicinity from 2008-2010.

Dr. Knox is a License Professional Counselor; he is currently an Adjunct Professor at Ashland Theological Seminary and Professor/Mentor at Ecumenical Theological Seminary. He also serves as Chaplain for Compassionate Care Hospice. Lastly Dr. Knox is married to the lovely Dranoel Aprol Knox; the father of their three beautiful children Saran Kenya, Rakahn Jamal, and Siedah Dranoel, and grandfather of Bria Johneshia and Jeremiah Marquise.

CPSIA information can be obtained at www.ICGtesting.com
Printed in the USA
BVOW060008260412

288680BV00004B/8/P